IS THAT MY PENIS

THE UNOFFICIAL PENIS BOOK OF RECORDS

by Dr. Jack Parry

Research & Editing by Sebastian & Joseph Parry

PARRY STUDIOS
Melbourne

Is that MY penis?

COPYRIGHT © 2024 JACK PARRY
(all rights reserved)

Parry Studios
Melbourne, Australia
Email: info@parrystudios.com

First published by Parry Studios 2024

Without limiting the rights under copyright reserved above, no part of this publication may be reproduced, stored in or introduced into a retrieval system, or transmitted, in any form or by any means (electronic, mechanical, photocopying, recording or otherwise) without the prior written permission of both the copyright owner and the above publisher of this book.

Research and editing by Joseph Parry and Sebastian Parry

Book design, illustrations and book cover by Jack Parry

Parry, Jack, 1972 -

ISBN 978-1-7638275-1-6

Parry, Jack, 1972 - ; Comic books, graphic novels, fotonovelas, cartoons, caricatures, comic strips

741.560

A catalogue record for this book is available from the National Library of Australia

www.parrystudios.com

NO........IT'S TOO LONG!

BUNGEEEEEE!

BARNACLE
(cirripedia)

The barnacle's penis is almost 8 times[1] longer than its body, making it, relative to its body size, the biggest and **longest** in the animal kingdom.

Is that MY penis?

NO........IT'S TOO SPIKY!

DOMESTIC CAT
(felis catus)

The domestic cat's penis is covered with small painful **spiky barbs**[2], which explains all the late night **cat**erwauling!

MeoooOOUCH!

Is that MY penis?

NO..........IT'S TOO CURLY!

DUCK
(anatinae)

The duck is one of the few birds with a penis. It also just happens to be very long, dangly and winds up just like a telephone cord when not in use.[3]

The Lake Duck (oxyura vittata) apparently has the longest penis of a vertebrate relative to its own body length, sometimes being as long as its own body.[4]

NO.........IT'S TOO HANDY!

DOLPHIN
(delphinus delphis)
The dolphin has a dual function penis. It is both retractable, rotatable and has a hook like structure on its end that it can grab and clasp onto females with!

NO.....IT'S TOO NOISY!

PYGMY WATER BOATMAN
(corixidae micronecta)

The Pygmy Water Boatman rubs its penis against its chest making an ear piercing sound that, relative to it size, is the **loudest** sound in the animal kingdom (99.2 decibels).[6]

Is that MY penis?

NO............IT'S TOO BOUNCY!

AMERICAN ALLIGATOR
(alligator mississippiensis)
The alligator has a highly collagenic penis[7] that is attached to its body by a **elastic cord** which flicks it out and back into its cloaca at high speed.

THAT'S NOT A KNIFE THIS IS A KNIFE!

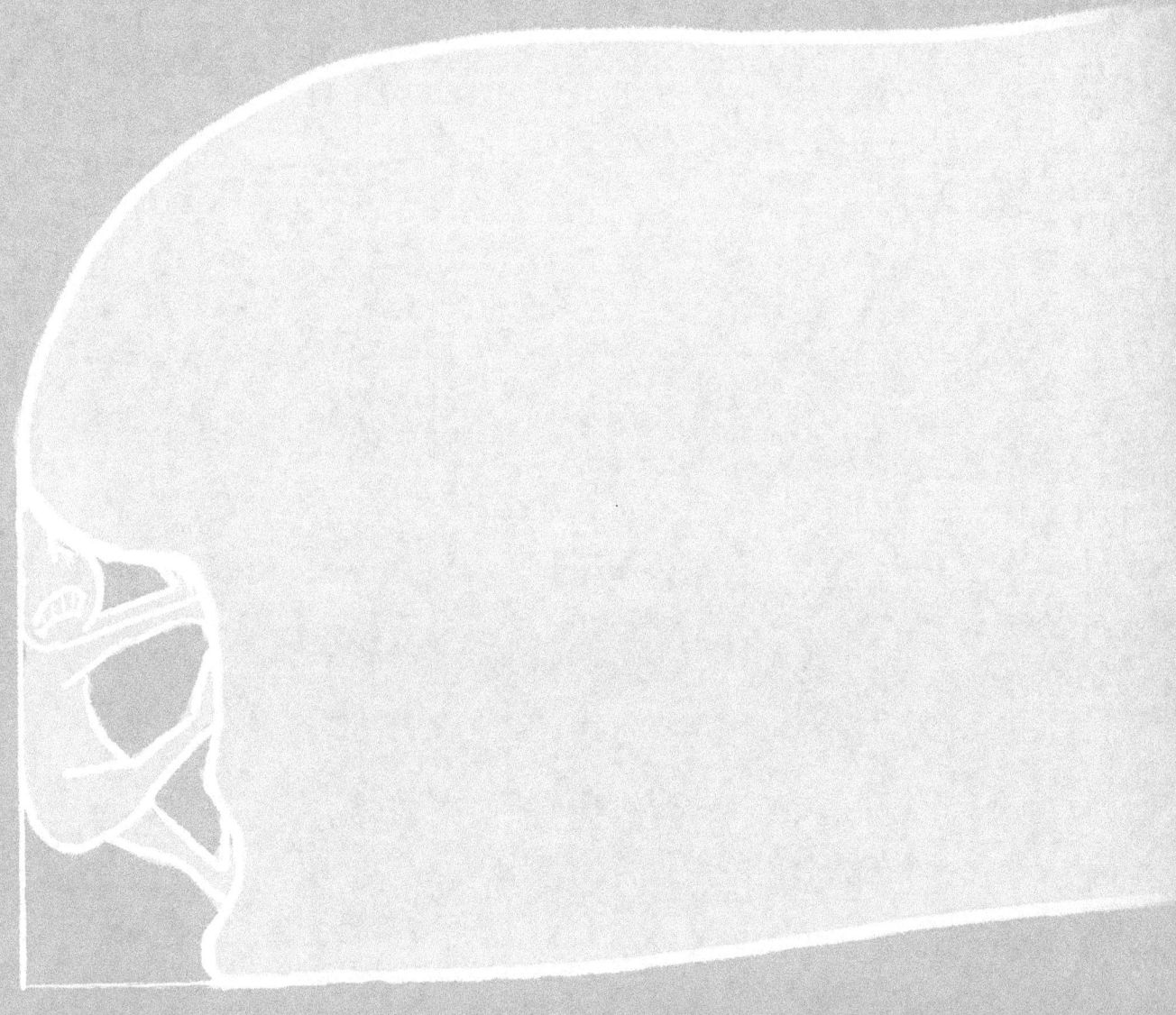

NO.........IT'S TOO ENORMOUS!

BLUE WHALE
(*balaenoptera musculus*)
The blue whale has the largest penis in the animal kingdom. It averages 2.4 - 3 metres long (8-10 feet).[8]

NO....IT'S TOO SILLY!

PHALLOSTETHUS CUULONG
(phallostethus cuulong)

The Phallostethus Cuulong is a recently discovered skinny, almost transparent fish that has its **penis on its head** ... that's right, a natural dickhead!

NO........IT'S TOO EXPLOSIVE!

HONEY BEE

(apis)

The drone honey bee only mates <u>once</u> then dies... This is because its nether regions literally **detonate**, snapping off in a violent **explosion**, leaving them plugged inside the queen.[10]

Is that MY penis?

NO.....ITS TOO DOWNUNDER!

EASTERN GREY KANGAROO
(macropus giganteus)

The kangaroo has a bifurcated[11] (twisty two shafted) penis that, **like Australia**, is **down-under!**

Its testes sit **above** its penis.

Is that MY penis?

NO.........................IT'S TOO INDEPENDENT!

"DON'T STAY OUT TOO LATE"

ARGONAUT OCTOPUS
(argonauta argo)

The Argonaut Octopus has a **removable penis**[12] which looks for a female all by itself. Females collect them and may even have their **favourites!**

Is that MY penis?

NO......IT'S TOO POINTY!

ELEPHANT
(loxodonta)

The elephant not only has the biggest penis of all land animals, it also has full control over where it points, giving it a very dexterous phallus.[13]

NO.....IT'S TOO PAINFUL!

SEAHORSE
(hippocampus)

The male seahorse is impregnated by the female seahorse.

When the babies are ready to be born, the male seahorse gives birth....

THROUGH HIS PENIS![14]

NO... IT'S TOO TINY!

POLAR BEAR
(ursus maritimus)

Male polar bears not only have to worry about the polar caps shrinking, but also their own penises![15]

Is that MY penis?

NO............IT'S TOO POPPY!

SHARK
(selachimorpha)

The shark has two penises called **CLASPERS**.[16] When one is fully extended it pops open like an umbrella!

A useful underwater addition...

Is that MY penis?

NO................IT'S TOO DEADLY!

BEAN WEEVIL
(callosobruchus maculatus)

The bean weevil's horrific penis is too frightening for words. It mates by puncturing the female with its barbs.[17]

A fatal attraction...

Is that MY penis?

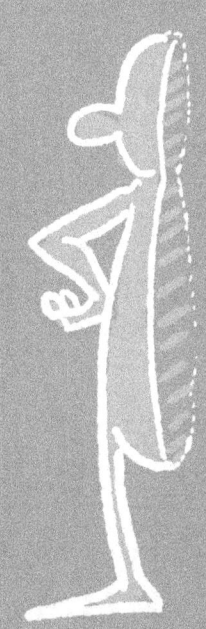
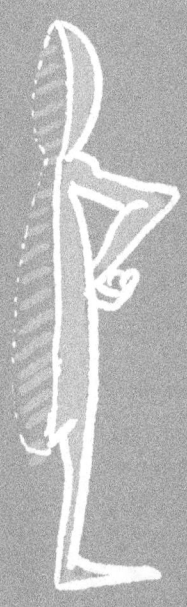

NO................IT'S TOO DIVIDED!

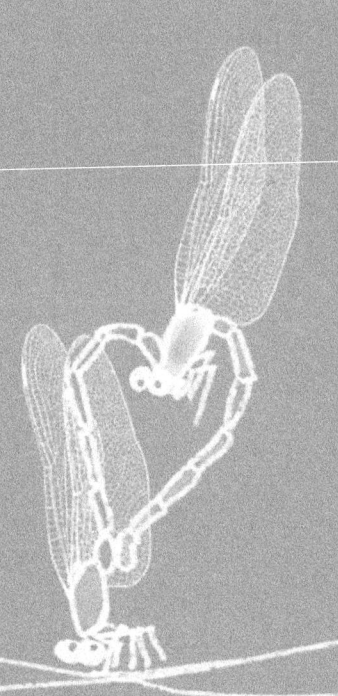

DRAGONFLY
(anisoptera)

The dragonfly has its penis split into two parts: the first part in its thorax and the second part on the tip of its tail![18]

Is that MY penis?

NO............IT'S TOO TASTY!

BANANA SLUG

(ariolimax)

Banana slugs are hermaphrodites and have been observed turning on each other during mating and trying to chew off their mate's penis![19]

Is that MY penis?

NO..............IT'S TOO BRUTAL!

FLATWORM
(pseudobiceros)

Flatworms engage in penis fencing using a two headed dagger-like penis. The flatworm who stabs the other first becomes the daddy![20]

NO..........................IT'S TOO REUSABLE!

SEA SLUG
(*goniobranchus reticulatus*)

The sea slug has a penis that it can detatch, regrow and then reuse! [21]

It can regrow a new penis **every day**

Is that MY penis?

Is that MY penis?

NO.................IT'S TOO TWISTY!

LEOPARD SLUG
(limax maximus)

The Leopard Slug has a blue tinted penis that pops out of its head.

It is so big that the hemaphrodite pair have to **spend hours** performing a slow twisting upside down manoeuvre just to support the sheer collective weight of their penises![23]

The ritual impregnates both of them, and they go off and lay about a hundred eggs afterwards.

NO............IT'S TOO DIRECT!

GARDEN SNAIL
(cornu aspersum)

The Garden Snail is a hemaphrodite that decides gender by shooting its partner's genitals (located in their head) with a small arrow - known as a **love dart**.

The best shot gets to be the man...[30]

Is that MY penis?

NO............IT'S TOO EDIBLE!

WASP SPIDER
(argiope bruennichi)

The Wasp Spider, in order to avoid being eaten by the female, chooses instead to amputate some, or all, of their own penises (called pedipalps),[25] for the female to snack on...

Is that MY penis?

NO............IT'S TWO HEADED!

PYTHON
(Pythonidae)

The Python has a two headed penis with one teste per penis.[26] This allows the python to keep shooting while his first gun reloads!

NO............IT'S TOO SHARP!

PIRATE BUG
(anthocoridae)

The Pirate Bug has a razor sharp penis that it uses to attack and stab the female pirate bug who usually dies from its wounds, just after giving birth![27]

Is that MY penis?

NO.....................IT'S TOO SCREWY!

PIG
(sus)

The Pig has a cork-screw shaped penis that screws into the female and is impossible to remove until he is ready...[28]

Is that MY penis?

NO......................IT'S TOO DELICIOUS!

ORB SPIDER
(nephilengys malabarensis)

The Orb Spider detaches its penis to avoid being eaten.

He's graced with two penises (on either side of his head), so he can offer her dessert too![29]

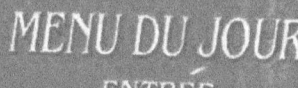

MENU DU JOUR
ENTRÉE
fricassee of penis

MAIN
Araneidae Soup

DESSERT
Penis à la mode

GULP?

Is that MY penis?

NO..................IT'S TOO WHIRLY!

"CONTROL TOWER...... REQUESTING PERMISSION TO LAND"

ECHIDNA
(tachyglossidae)

The echidna has...

A ROTATING FOUR-HEADED PENIS![24]

...making it clearly the most unusual penis of all!

Is that MY penis?

YES! THAT'S MY PENIS!

HUMAN
(Homo Sapiens)

The human penis isn't:

Long, spiky, curly, handy, noisy, bouncy, enormous, silly, explosive, upside-down, liberated, pointy, painful, tiny, poppy, dangerous, divided, tasty, brutal, reusable, floral, twisty, whirly, edible, two-headed, sharp, screwy, delicious or direct...

In fact, its probably the most un-interesting, un-remarkable penis in the animal kingdom...

Just boring really...

Is that MY penis?

REFERENCES

1. Christopher J Neufeld and A. Richard Palmer, 'Precisely Proportioned: Intertidal Barnacles Alter Penis Form to Suit Coastal Wave Action', Proceedings of the Royal Society B: Biological Sciences 275, no. 1638 (7 May 2008): 1081–87, https://doi.org/10.1098/rspb.2007.1760.
2. Lester R. Aronson and Madeline L. Cooper, 'Penile Spines of the Domestic Cat: Their Endocrine-behavior Relations', The Anatomical Record 157, no. 1 (January 1967): 71–78, https://doi.org/10.1002/ar.1091570111.
3. Adam Marcus, 'Ostrich Penis Clears up Evolutionary Mystery', Nature, 8 December 2011, nature.2011.9600, https://doi.org/10.1038/nature.2011.9600.
4. Kevin G. McCracken, 'The 20-Cm Spiny Penis of the Argentine Lake Duck (Oxyura Vittata)', The Auk 117, no. 3 (1 July 2000): 820–25, https://doi.org/10.1093/auk/117.3.820.
5. Dara N. Orbach et al., 'Genital Interactions during Simulated Copulation among Marine Mammals', Proceedings of the Royal Society B: Biological Sciences 284, no. 1864 (11 October 2017): 20171265, https://doi.org/10.1098/rspb.2017.1265.
6. Jérôme Sueur, David Mackie, and James F. C. Windmill, 'So Small, So Loud: Extremely High Sound Pressure Level from a Pygmy Aquatic Insect (Corixidae, Micronectinae)', ed. Daphne Soares, PLoS ONE 6, no. 6 (15 June 2011): e21089, https://doi.org/10.1371/journal.pone.0021089.
7. D.A. Kelly, 'Penile Anatomy and Hypotheses of Erectile Function in the American Alligator (Alligator Mississippiensis): Muscular Eversion and Elastic Retraction', The Anatomical Record 296, no. 3 (March 2013): 488–94, https://doi.org/10.1002/ar.22644.
8. Alan F. Dixson, Mammalian Sexuality: The Act of Mating and the Evolution of Reproduction: Appendix 3A - Penile Lengths in Mammals, 1st ed. (Cambridge University Press, 2021), https://doi.org/10.1017/9781108550758.
9. Koichi Shibukawa, Dinh Dac Tran, and Loi Xuan Tran, 'Phallostethus Cuulong, a New Species of Priapiumfish (Actinopterygii: Atheriniformes: Phallostethidae) from the Vietnamese Mekong', Zootaxa 3363, no. 1 (3 July 2012), https://doi.org/10.11646/zootaxa.3363.1.3.
10. Benjamin P. Oldroyd and Siriwat Wongsiri, Asian Honey Bees: Biology, Conservation, and Human Interactions (Cambridge, Mass: Harvard University Press, 2006).
11. Natalie M. Warburton, Philip W. Bateman, and Patricia A. Fleming, 'Anatomy of the Cavernous Muscles of the Kangaroo Penis Highlights Marsupial–Placental Dichotomy', Journal of Anatomy 234, no. 3 (March 2019): 306–15, https://doi.org/10.1111/joa.12930.
12. Giambattista Bello, 'Evolution of the Hectocotylus in Sepiolinae (Cephalopoda: Sepiolidae) and Description of Four New Genera', European Journal of Taxonomy, no. 655 (29 May 2020), https://doi.org/10.5852/ejt.2020.655.
13. Elephant Scratches His Belly With His Penis, 2015, https://www.youtube.com/watch?v=T1rcoTGWnWg.
14. Glenn I Moore, 'Reproductive Biology of the Western Australian Seahorse Hippocampus Subelongatus' (Unpublished, 2001), https://doi.org/10.13140/2.1.1787.2165.

Is that MY penis?

REFERENCES (Continued)

15. Christian Sonne et al., 'Xenoendocrine Pollutants May Reduce Size of Sexual Organs in East Greenland Polar Bears (Ursus Maritimus)', Environmental Science & Technology 40, no. 18 (1 September 2006): 5668–74, https://doi.org/10.1021/es060836n.
16. John R. F. Dick, 'Sphenacanthus, a Palaeozoic Freshwater Shark', Zoological Journal of the Linnean Society 122, no. 1–2 (January 1998): 9–25, https://doi.org/10.1111/j.1096-3642.1998.tb02523.x.
17. Bean Beetle Reveals Prickly Penis before Violent Sex, 2015, https://www.youtube.com/watch?v=zY6qtIIyM-LE.
18. P. L. Miller, 'The Structure and Function of the Genitalia in the Libellulidae (Odonata)', Zoological Journal of the Linnean Society 102, no. 1 (May 1991): 43–73, https://doi.org/10.1111/j.1096-3642.1991.tb01536.x.
19. H Reise, 'Penis-Biting Slugs: Wild Claims and Confusions', Trends in Ecology & Evolution 17, no. 4 (1 April 2002): 163, https://doi.org/10.1016/S0169-5347(02)02453-9.
20. Carla Vreys and Nico K Michiels, 'Sperm Trading by Volume in a Hermaphroditic Flatworm with Mutual Penis Intromission', Animal Behaviour 56, no. 3 (September 1998): 777–85, https://doi.org/10.1006/anbe.1998.0829.
21. Ayami Sekizawa et al., 'Disposable Penis and Its Replenishment in a Simultaneous Hermaphrodite', Biology Letters 9, no. 2 (23 April 2013): 20121150, https://doi.org/10.1098/rsbl.2012.1150.
22. G. R. Zug, 'The Penial Morphology and the Relationships of Cryptodiran Turtles', 1966, http://deepblue.lib.umich.edu/handle/2027.42/57083.
23. IUCN, 'Limax Maximus: Rowson, B.: The IUCN Red List of Threatened Species 2017: E.T170900A85577040', 20 June 2016, https://doi.org/10.2305/IUCN.UK.2017-3.RLTS.T170900A85577040.en.
24. S. D. Johnston et al., 'One-Sided Ejaculation of Echidna Sperm Bundles', The American Naturalist 170, no. 6 (December 2007): E162–64, https://doi.org/10.1086/522847.
25. Menno Schilthuizen, 'The Nihilistic Sex Lives of Spiders', Slate, 10 June 2014, https://slate.com/technology/2014/06/spider-sex-why-male-spiders-intentionally-castrate-themselves-during-copulation.html.
26. Francisca Leal and Martin J. Cohn, 'Development of Hemipenes in the Ball Python Snake Python Regius', Sexual Development 9, no. 1 (2015): 6–20, https://doi.org/10.1159/000363758.
27. Amy Backhouse, Steven M. Sait, and Tom C. Cameron, 'Multiple Mating in the Traumatically Inseminating Warehouse Pirate Bug, Xylocoris Flavipes: Effects on Fecundity and Longevity', Biology Letters 8, no. 5 (23 October 2012): 706–9, https://doi.org/10.1098/rsbl.2012.0091.
28. Peter Jackson and Peter Cockcroft, 'Clinical Examination of the Pig', In Practice 27, no. 2 (February 2005): 93–102, https://doi.org/10.1136/inpract.27.2.93.
29. Daiqin Li et al., 'Remote Copulation: Male Adaptation to Female Cannibalism', Biology Letters 8, no. 4 (23 August 2012): 512–15, https://doi.org/10.1098/rsbl.2011.1202.
30. M Schilthuizen, 'The Darting Game in Snails and Slugs', Trends in Ecology & Evolution 20, no. 11 (November 2005): 581–84, https://doi.org/10.1016/j.tree.2005.08.014.

www.ingramcontent.com/pod-product-compliance
Lightning Source LLC
Chambersburg PA
CBHW082247090526
44585CB00021BA/2479